Counseling on

Early Sexual Memories

Counseling on
Early Sexual Memories

— *Joan Karp*

Sex can be a wonderful way of getting close to another human being. It can be an expression of love and caring, an experience of safety and intimacy. It can make life richer, warmer, easier. It can help a person remember the truly benign nature of human beings. Sex can be a place where each partner can show herself or himself more fully than usual and experience being accepted and loved deeply. Sex can be fun.

Unfortunately, most people do not experience sex in this way very often, if ever. In order to experience even some of the benefits of sex, people will endure many difficulties, overlook many unsolved problems. Others find it easier to be close to loved ones without sex; they lack the resources to make the sexual part of the relationship work well enough.

It appears that almost everyone has been badly hurt in the area of sex. ("Abusers" are simply people who were badly abused as children themselves.)

Sex is not as important as it is made to seem. However, capitalist societies manipulate people to keep them preoccupied with sex, to keep them feeling bad about themselves, and to keep them buying products they wouldn't want otherwise.

Human beings need closeness, touching, and loving. In present societies people are taught that sex is the only acceptable way to fully meet these needs. However, these needs can be met without sex. Many Co-Counselors' experience has been that as they become able to cuddle, touch and be close, often with many people in their lives, preoccupation with sex diminishes or disappears. Thus sex loses much of its false "importance."

Difficulties with sex are also an indication of unhealed hurts. These hurts often impose severe limitations on other areas of our functioning. Hurts in the area of sex can affect our sense of power, well-being, confidence, trust, creativity, and physical mobility along with our ability to choose, to desire, to think clearly, to set up good relationships, to be close. Thus full recovery of one's complete humanness requires discharging the distresses which have become attached to sex.

COUNSELING ON THE EARLIEST MEMORY

"What is your earliest memory connected to sex in any way at all?" Answering this question can start unravelling a lifetime of distress which has somehow become connected to sex.

Co-Counselors have found that releasing the tensions (through talking, crying, laughing, etc.)

connected with one's earliest memory in a particular area of difficulty, is an efficient way to begin work in that area.

In identifying our earliest sexual memory, uncensored "first thoughts" can be reliable. In a particular memory, the relationship to sex is often obscure at first. However, seemingly insignificant memories often turn out to be important.

Why is it helpful to work on the earliest remembered incident? Focusing on these early incidents leads to important insights about leftover distress recordings which have confused us about reality ever since they were installed.

It is useful to review the nature of distress recordings. When our intelligences are working properly, we take in huge amounts of information from the environment, evaluate it, and store it for future use in discrete bits which can be retrieved separately. We use this stored information collected by our senses to create successful responses to new situations. We compare and contrast each new situation to any relevant information "on file" in our brains. This enables us, depending on the amount of already stored information, to determine an accurate, flexible course of action.

When we receive information while we are hurting, either physically or emotionally, our intelligences do not work properly. Instead the sensory input "mis-stores," creating what acts like a literal "recording" of the entire hurtful incident. This includes feelings of distress and difficulty in thinking.

When recordings are restimulated, we may "think" (on either an aware or an unaware level), "Something is wrong here," "I am no good," "You are no good," "This is too much for me," "All people wearing red shirts will hurt me," "Bad things happen on hot days," and so on, depending on the exact nature of the original hurtful experience.

In this way, early incidents of distress lay the groundwork for how later experiences are perceived and handled. For example, a victim may "tolerate" sexual abuse because of recordings from earlier hurts, such as "I deserve mistreatment" or "help is not available."

This phenomenon can be commonly observed in a classroom environment. Imagine a situation where a teacher, having a hard time, yells harshly at the entire class of students. Objectively, each student has experienced almost exactly the same thing. Each does not feel the same way, however, about what she has experienced. The wide range of reactions might include getting angry, being terrified, feeling victimized "again," blaming oneself, trying to "fix" the situation, or simply understanding that the teacher was having a hard day, without experiencing any restimulation of bad feelings at all. In each case, prior hurtful experiences or the absence of them, affected how this incident was experienced.

Once a person has been hurt in a particular way, he tends to become rigid and tense, expecting to be treated badly again in the same way rather than being free to respond flexibly to the actual situation. This tense behavior can then actually cause future difficulties.

This phenomenon is sufficient explanation for many difficulties in relationships. For example, a child who is treated very harshly each time she takes a bath (by a parent who was treated harshly while taking baths as a child) is likely to be tense and feeling badly whenever she is in a bathtub. Imagine that child being invited to share a bath at a friend's house. Feeling upset and tense, she might pick a fight or have other difficulties with her friend. She unawarely brings these old feelings into a new and different situation in hopes of being able to discharge them. Distress recordings thus leave us vulnerable to confusion. Without a strong decision to keep thinking, we tend to respond to a new situation by re-enacting the original distress-filled incident.

Each time we are unsuccessful in handling a similar incident, we add another layer of restimulation. Counseling on the earliest memory related to sex in any way will enable re-evaluation not only of that particular incident but also of later incidents that are connected in some way to the earlier one.

Discharging the distress in the earliest sexual memory to completion will lead to relaxed remembering of all the details of that experience. Then one can go on to the next later incident that can be remembered. However, when persistent discharge leads to remembering an earlier memory first, clients can work on that incident instead.

It is also helpful to review and discharge very hurtful incidents which occurred considerably later in one's life. This includes sexual abuse. Working on one's earliest sexual memory is not a substitute for working on the later incidents, even though it will make it easier to recover from the later incidents. (Using the role-exchange technique can be especially effective in recovering from any experiences of sexual abuse. See the following article.)

Focusing on present-day feelings related to sex has usually not worked well in our experience. Almost everyone is deeply confused in the area of sex. If a counselor is confused about reality, he will not perceive the distress accurately and the contradictions he thinks of are likely to be inaccurate also. Counselors are less likely to be confused about a client's *earlier* incidents; they can probably provide more accurate contradictions.

Another reason for beginning work on sexual distresses with the earliest memories is that in these early experiences sexism was usually not overtly present. Both boys and girls were victimized in very similar ways. If one begins to work on later sexual experiences first, the restimulation is likely to confuse both male and female counselors.

The client may discharge some when talking about present-day feelings, but there will tend to be less re-evaluation than occurs with discharge on an early incident. If, however, the main bulk of the distress has been unloaded from the earliest-remembered incident, the Co-Counselors can come to the adult experiences with much more awareness.

Recounting sexual fantasies (whether current or from childhood) can also be a direct route to discharging recordings that included sexual arousal. If sexual arousal is present during an experience of hurt (whether or not the arousal is directly related to the hurt), then sexual arousal will become part of the distress recording. Sexual fantasies (masturbation fantasies) are restimulations of these earlier distresses.

Counseling on distresses related to sex has worked best in small groups of four or five people involving both men and women. Effective work can also be done in two-way sessions and other types of groups.

The feelings present during the early hurtful incident (e.g. discouragement, desperation, confusion) tend to influence how people feel about working on early sexual memories. For example, if a major early incident had a component of being over-powered, this feeling will tend to attach itself to the present situation when one tries to address this incident, and it may seem overwhelming to work on it. Similarly, it is possible for a client to become preoccupied with working on sexual distress, and assume the compulsive attitude toward counseling on sex that was formerly connected to sex itself. These feelings need to be contradicted.

Support groups themselves sometimes feel like they will "go on forever" (like the original incidents seemed to have done). Successful support groups have sometimes convened for a limited number of sessions for this reason, re-forming or not as the participants decide.

Groups may also need to periodically invite an experienced counselor to be a guest leader, and to occasionally work on the relationships between the group members, to keep the group moving well.

(See Notes/Reminders/Helpful Hints For Support Group Leaders at the end of this article. Also see Harvey Jackins' pamphlet, "A Rational Theory of Sexuality" for a more complete discussion of the theoretical basis of this work.)

OPPRESSION AND SEXUAL DISTRESS

Sex plays different roles in different oppressions. What follows are some generalizations about the role that sex can play in several oppressions. These observations may be useful to members of these groups and to allies if we also keep in mind that each person's experiences are entirely unique and "one-of-a-kind."

FEMALES AND SEX

Sex is used as a tool of the oppression of females. Rape is the extreme case. Sexism is acted out in many ways in sexual encounters between men and women—for example, objectification of women's bodies, lack of attention to women's lives and concerns, and the traditional assumption that the man's sexual "needs" are of primary importance. Also, women's natural appreciation of their own bodies, as well as men's bodies, has been interfered with by the oppression.

Many women never experience sex without either actual sexual exploitation or the restimulation of feelings from past sexual exploitation. Thus women are often left feeling like victims whether or not the actual situation is exploitative. Women need encouragement to step out of these feelings of victimization, to stop defending them, and to take charge and set up enjoyable lives and relationships on their terms. Women have to contradict the "Prince Charming" myth, encouraged by society, which reinforces passivity by promising they will have an ideal relationship without having to take any initiative.

MALES AND SEX

Sex plays a very different role in the oppression of men than in the oppression of women. Denial of closeness and caring is a key feature of male oppression. Sex is one of the few ways men have been allowed to be close to another human being. Thus sex, especially when it is combined with closeness and caring, looks to many men like their only opportunity to contradict the loneliness and isolation of their oppression. Because of this, sex can take on a desperate "importance" to men.

The oppressive society has "invented" all oppressions, including men's oppression, to maintain its exploitative role in human affairs. Thus the society encourages men to fantasize about the perfect sexual encounter. This functions to distract men from their isolation and loneliness. (If men's isolation were actually eliminated, it would no longer be possible to maintain other aspects of men's oppression; thus freed, men would probably move quickly to eliminate the oppressive society.) A compulsive "interest" in sex plays a key role in keeping men isolated and therefore more able to play an oppressive role towards others. It also becomes a barrier to creating the close, caring relationships they actually want.

Other aspects of men's oppression include being made to feel that they are bad for being male, for having sexual distresses, and especially for ever having acted them out. Men often feel that they must protect others from themselves. This makes it particularly difficult for many men to Co-Counsel effectively in this area.

LESBIANS, GAY MEN AND BI-SEXUALS

Sexual behavior is the excuse for the oppression of Lesbians, Gay men, and bisexuals, not the reason for it. The oppression of Lesbians, Gay men and bisexuals is used to threaten all people into acting "normally" to avoid being labeled as "Gay." Gay oppression divides people so that they will not join together and end the economic exploitation of the majority of the population.

Society says that Gay and Lesbian sexual distresses and behaviors are "far worse" than those of non-Gays, and that those who carry them are "deserving of mistreatment." Because the sexual behaviors of Gay and Lesbian people are the excuse for the oppression, many members of this group feel defensive and under attack in this area. This needs to be understood so as not to reinforce this oppression. It especially needs to be understood to successfully counsel Gay men, Lesbians, and bisexuals on distress connected with sex.

INCEST SURVIVORS

Incest survivors have a special relationship to sexual distresses. They were often abused by people they trusted and loved and upon whom they were often dependent. Thus, they are particularly vulnerable to confusion in this area.

If incest survivors, in turn, have passed on the distress recording by abusing younger siblings or neighbors, or children of their own, it can be especially difficult to work on that person's own hurts because of the shame and guilt that the person is likely to feel.

In counseling incest survivors, effective contradictions must often be found first to pretence, which began with pretending that the incest wasn't really happening, but by now often affects everything in the person's life.

Incest survivors often have particular difficulty in trusting others and in resisting "caretaking" roles. Contradictions need to be found to both these distresses in order for the client to fully use his or her counselor.

Incest survivors often need encouragement to take charge and not fearfully demand changes in others under the guise of "taking charge." (Rather than really taking charge, there is often a pull to blame others for their "restimulating behavior" and demand that they change their behavior. This is not the same as taking charge.) Contradictions are needed rather than "sympathy," as well as encouragment not to settle for limitations in their lives.

Incest survivors often feel uniquely abused, perhaps because of the "taboo" nature of the mistreatment. This feeling needs to be looked at and challenged.

After sufficient discharge has occurred on early hurts, a person will tend, spontaneously, to turn her or his attention to present-time concerns. However, some people may eventually need some extra encouragement to let go of the distress (i.e. to give up their "identity" as an incest survivor) as a necessary step in fully recovering from the original hurts.

Parents' oppression is a factor in incest. Isolation and exhaustion are key features of parents' oppression, especially for the parents of very young children. Under these conditions, parents are more vulnerable to acting out their distresses. Also, because the society leads adults to believe that very young children will not remember what happened to them, acting out sexual and other distress at one's children can be more easily rationalized.

JEWS

For Jewish children, distresses from sexual abuse often overlap closely with the recordings installed by internalized oppression. Experiences of sexual abuse may tend to simply confirm the message that the world is not safe for Jews. Also, much of internalized Jewish oppression is passed on in Jewish families under the guise of (usually patterned) love and closeness ("you are safe only if you are close to us"). This perpetuates a pretense that bad things do not happen within Jewish families and can make it difficult to get help for abusive situations.

CATHOLICS

Many Catholics were made to feel unworthy and bad about themselves. Many are taught that any thoughts or feelings related to sex with anyone but a spouse is not just bad but will lead to "eternal damnation." Therefore, it can be especially scary to work in this area. In addition, the body is usually focused on as a vehicle for sacrifice and suffering, not for enjoyment. For many Catholics, working lightly on heavy embarrassment opens access to other distresses. (For racial and ethnic groups which are primarily Catholic, these issues can exist in the culture as a whole.)

BLACK PEOPLE

Historically, sexual restimulation has been used to oppress black people in the United States and elsewhere. The dehumanizing ideology of slavery in the United States included an image of black men as "sexual animals." Lynchings, although most often motivated by economic factors, such as to intimidate sharecroppers out of organizing for better conditions, were often publicly attributed to attempted rapes of white women. Whites have been conditioned to believe these myths and are vulnerable to restimulation in this way. This leaves many black men feeling that it is dangerous to show their distresses in this area.

The tradition under slavery of expected submission of any black woman to any white male still persists underground in the sexist male culture, along with the attitude that black women are exotic.

Other pressures related to the oppression can make it seem frivolous to put attention on what feels like a purely personal issue of sexual distress.

CHINESE AND JAPANESE PEOPLE

It has served the oppressive societies in which Chinese people and Japanese people have been minorities, to propagandize that Chinese men and Japanese men are "asexual." Chinese and Japanese women, on the other hand, are often objectified as "exotic" and of special sexual interest by the majority culture.

In Chinese and Japanese cultures, it can be particularly important to uphold the good name of the family. This can mean that "family matters," including any sexual abuse, is kept strictly "within the family." This may reinforce the general tendency to occlude childhood abuse. In addition, talking about sex in any way is often considered improper. It can be especially useful to assist Chinese and Japanese Co-Counselors to discharge embarrassment in this area.

OWNING CLASS

Owning-class children are often treated harshly as preparation for their future oppressive roles in society. The scarcity of real human caring and closeness in many owning-class families makes these children especially vulnerable to ongoing sexual victimization by adults or other young people because the physical closeness of the interactions, although abusive, may provide welcome relief from the otherwise heavy isolation.

There are many, many other groups which also have a unique relationship to sexual distress.

Understanding how these larger factors operate may make it easier for each person to fully recover from her or his own particular set of distresses.

GUIDES FOR ACTION

While recovering from sexual distresses, there are several things to keep in mind. First, **"Almost everything that any one of us has assumed to be natural or inherent in the area of our sexuality is recorded distress patterns."** (Harvey Jackins, "Toward a Rational Theory of Sexuality")

Not only have we been hurt in this area, but we have been encouraged to act on our feelings without making any distinction between those which are based on distress and those which are not. Discharge and re-evaluation of early sexual distresses is the only reliable way to gain insight into the difference. Any assumptions which have not been re-evaluated in this way are suspect.

There is a fundamental difference between actions based on rationality (and the attempt to think) and actions determined by distress recordings. With the former, a person remains essentially in charge of the situation, even if it does not turn out well and distresses are played out. Mistakes can be evaluated, difficulties understood, new information assimilated. Actions based on distress recordings, however, have no such advantages. It is a defeat for the human who has been trapped yet again in a familiar and dependably unworkable situation. All involved are victimized by the pattern, flexible thinking is not a component, and the person is left without a contradiction to the early feelings.

As in every other area of our lives, it does not make sense to base our actions on our feelings, but rather on our best thinking. This is true, even though we have been taught that we are not supposed to think in the areas of love and sex, and have been systematically manipulated by many sources into acting on our feelings.

(The word "feelings" is used with a variety of meanings—natural "feelings" of well-being, etc.; distressed, recorded "feelings" which are usually negative but can seem positive; sexual "feelings" which are defined here as a combination of physical and emotional elements, and which can be based on distress but don't have to be.)

UNBIDDEN SEXUAL FEELINGS

"Unbidden sexual feelings are restimulation." (Harvey Jackins, "Toward a Rational Theory of Sexuality") Any time a person experiences sexual arousal *without first having decided to*, it is almost certainly a restimulation of an old distress recording which contains sexual feelings.

These physical responses are attached to recordings of emotional distress, which can seem "negative" or "positive" in flavor. Most people rely on knowing how to restimulate sexual arousal in themselves and others in "socially acceptable" ways when they engage in sex. ("If you speak in this tone of voice, if the room is lit in this way, if we walk on a beautiful beach, etc., I will become sexually aroused." See Jackins' article for discussion of "non-socially acceptable" triggers.) Without distress, two people who love each other very much can cuddle and hold each other close, skin to skin, without sexual feelings, unless they decide otherwise.

AN AWARE CHOICE

We can ultimately have control over sexual feelings. Meanwhile, we can decide whether or not to act on any sexual feelings we may have. An aware choice can be made about whether and when to add sex to any particular relationship. For many people, this brings to mind a cumbersome process of many sessions, consultations, list-making of pros and cons, and so on, before deciding to have sex. This might not be a bad idea for a while, but people can eventually develop good judgment which they can learn to call upon quickly and easily.

It seems that without distress, human beings experience a relaxed desire for sex in some situations. (Sex can be an elegant way of being close to someone you care about when everything else makes sense.)

There seems to be an instinctive survival drive towards sex inherited from our pre-intelligent forebears, which exists after adolescence. (There is also an instinctive high-priority survival drive in our human heritage attached to eating, which operates from birth onwards.) As with all inherited instinctive drives for humans, these come under the control and management of our intelligence unless distress patterns become attached to them. In our societies distress patterns are almost systematically attached to these instincts about sex and food through the operation of the patterned cultures. (This may be why addictions and other patterns that become attached to sex and food have been so difficult to discharge in Co-Counseling. The patterns, once present, draw strength from the physiological mechanisms of the pre-rational instinctive drives.)

Most societies have made it very difficult for people to distinguish between a desire for love, touching, and closeness and a desire for sex. Needs for love, touching, and closeness are very real and large, yet most people have been taught that these needs can only be met through sex. Judging what makes sense in a given situation is much easier if you can tell whether you are actually interested in sex or if it is love and closeness which you want.

This explains a phenomenon which too many people are familiar with—deciding to have sex, and then feeling both good and bad "in the morning." Good because needs for touching and closeness, and maybe love as well, were met. Bad because meeting those needs involved rehearsing distresses related to sex one more time.

Often these real needs for love, touching, and closeness have become "frozen." Until the recorded feeling of need is discharged, a person may never feel sufficiently loved, for instance, regardless of the actual situation. Most people also have blocks on their ability to love, be close and initiate aware touching. The rational need to express love and to initiate aware closeness and touching seems to be greater than the rational need to receive them; thus, contrary to the way people often feel, there need be no actual shortage of love and closeness in the world.

Sex can function as the best contradiction to isolation for some people. During sex, people can notice that they are not alone, often discharging deep hurts, which for non-Co-Counselors (and many Co-Counselors) may be an unusual occurrence otherwise. Whether they realize it or not, they may seek out opportunities for sex as a form of needed reassurance and a way to keep their lives going well. The behavior may be combined with compulsions, but compulsive sexual behavior by itself does not offer any helpful contradictions. Without seeking closeness through other means, however, such sexual behavior may inadvertently reinforce the isolation it seeks to end.

SEXUAL "COMPULSIONS"

Sexual "compulsions," or addictive compulsive sexual behaviors, have often required great persistence and sharp counseling to overcome. As with food and eating, the process of trying to fill rational human needs, in this case for closeness and affection, can serve to solidify the distresses attached to them. Eating and sex also have physiological aspects which become additional parts of any distress recordings, further complicating the recovery process.

For most people overcoming sexual compulsions requires a combination of decision, solid work on early sexual memories and sexual fantasies, and reaching for real human closeness in the present. A key element is a decision to stop the addictive behavior, and to discharge whatever feelings come up in the absence of acting out the compulsion or in the attempt to stop acting it out. At the same time, consistent work on early sexual memories drains the restimulations feeding the compulsion, and assists the client to distinguish the present from the past.

In addition to efforts at ending isolation generally, people with compulsive sexual behavior need to reach for real human connections as a specific contradiction when the distress recordings try to take over.

It is important in the process of working on a sexual compulsion to discharge any feelings of shame for not having already overcome the addiction or for failing in repeated tries to overcome it; these feelings of shame will only increase the pull to repeat the compulsion. Also, a common mistake is to assume that the best contradiction to the shame is to celebrate and repeat the addiction.

MASTURBATION

Masturbation, continued past first experimentation with newly-awakened sexuality, seems to be the result of restimulated early distresses. Many people are quite clear that their urge to masturbate is compulsive. They may or may not understand what triggers the distress recording which includes this physical component, but they know their lives would be better without it. Others, however, are under the illusion that they are exercising a full choice in their behavior. Often the triggering recording involves a "determined decision" that "I deserve to feel good!"

The heavy, oppressive, and abusive interventions around masturbation often experienced by children leaves many people understandably suspicious of listening to any "authority" on this topic. Each person can determine for herself or himself whether there is a "trigger" which restimulates the urge to masturbate.

Many people have found that when they stopped acting on compulsive feelings to masturbate that they were able to discharge more fully and on a wider range of related distresses. Some people are able to notice that as long as they are discharging well on the hurts related to sexual abuse, they have no interest in masturbation. Other people, who have gone for long periods with no sexual feelings, have found experimenting with sexual feelings through masturbation to be helpful. (Children should not be interfered with when they masturbate. They are either exploring new body sensations or it is a symptom of other distresses which can be worked on at other times. Adults need to be especially aware of the pulls to pass on our own mistreatment in this area.)

HUMAN CONNECTION

Many people who find it difficult to experience a human connection during sex will choose to be celibate for a while. Until they can discharge more of the hurts in this area, whether inhibiting or compulsive, they decide to keep sex out of their relationships. They wait until they can predict some success in being close and taking charge in sexual relations. Some people, however, may decide they are very "comfortable" waiting, without continuing to challenge the distresses. They are possibly caught in acting out a different aspect of the distress, an early frozen "no," which is no longer useful. For these people, the challenge (if not always the actuality) of resuming sexual activity will keep both their sessions and their lives moving well.

STAYING IN "PRESENT TIME"

Early hurts in the area of sexuality do not have to completely determine current actions and attitudes. Especially after people counsel in this area for a while, they are often able to notice that they have the power to decide to be free of the influence of past distresses. Working to stay in "present time" can be an extremely important factor in the success of any close relationship, and especially a sexual one.

The pull of early feelings looking for a place to discharge can be particularly strong in the safety of an intimate relationship. However, even a victim of heavy early abuse does not have to wait until all of the distress is discharged before attempting to decide to enjoy sex (by keeping attention off of the old distress and in the present) and to take charge of any relationship.

In fact, complete recovery seems to require deciding and repeatedly deciding until it becomes possible to take a stand against the illusion of the distress in this way. (If this decision is attempted before a certain amount of counseling work has been done, however, it can fall into acting out the distress in a different form.)

In general, any sexual encounter will work best if the participants keep their attention in the present, unless an aware decision has been made for one or the other to become client. (Even then, things will often go better if the client discharges with their attention away from the distress.) If the action can be stopped when that is no longer possible, hopefully for some informal or formal counseling or other "attention out" activity, then everyone will "feel better in the morning" (even if you stop short of sex).

INHIBITION

Although most societies impose *compulsive* attitudes about sex on their populations, *inhibition* can also describe the relationship of many individuals to sex. Others experience some combination of compulsion and inhibition. Both are based on heavy early hurts.

Clients who have successfully discharged patterns of inhibition have combined consistent counseling on early memories and sexual fantasies with major challenges to their fears outside of session (for instance, a long, arduous bike trip), and a successful decision to keep their attention away from their distress. Choosing to keep attention off the old distresses during sex is essential, and can be combined with actually deciding to have sexual feelings. (For instance, take the direction, said eagerly out loud or silently, "Yes, I want sexual feelings!") Taking full charge in all areas, but especially being the initiator during sex and using your partner to help you enjoy yourself, are also important contradictions to the pull of past victimization.

Each person deserves to enjoy sex to the extent she or he wishes, but the inability to do so caused by inhibition is not a major problem in and of itself. Sex is not essential to our well-being, although closeness is. However, inhibition is an indication of distresses which also limit a person in other important ways, including the ability to be close. It is important to recover from the related distresses in order to lead a full life.

ATTRACTIONS

Repetitive attraction to people who are similar in some way, such as in body type, color of hair, way of speaking, etc., is based at least in part on restimulation. When this kind of "feeling" of attraction is rejected as a basis for pursuing a relationship, you are much more likely to be able to think about the person as a whole, including about whether or not you would like to be in a relationship with this person.

Attractions are not always based on restimulation, however. A human being is inherently attractive, and attraction can result from getting enough of a glimpse of a person's full humanness. Whether or not you decide to act on the attraction, it can provide important contradictions which can be useful to work on during Co-Counseling sessions. (Talk about everything you love about the person, what life would be like if you could live with him forever, what would earlier struggles have been like if she had been there. Describe in as much detail as you can manage your fantasies of sex with this person, usually with a counselor who is not the person you're attracted to. Before long, the connections with your early sexual distress will become apparent, and you can return to that focus as client.)

MAKING RELATIONSHIPS WORK WELL

Theoretically, to work well, relationships require only one person, *but at least one person* who has decided to take charge of the relationship and to make it work. There is often a pull to want that person to be the other person, but it might as well be you. Otherwise you are putting yourself in the position of agreeing to be a victim to someone else's patterns. In general terms, this also means resisting the urge to blame the other person. If you have no related difficulties, then a partner's patterns are usually easy to handle. It is also helpful to be explicit with each other about your expectations for the relationship and to understand where you do not agree about those expectations.

Actually taking charge of a relationship is not the same as an "in charge" pattern taking over. Actually taking charge may include having high expectations for the other person, including the amount of initiative taken, making requirements (with some picture of what it may take for the person to meet those requirements), and in general being totally flexible about what kind of a role you will play in order to make things go well. It also means understanding that there are difficulties on both sides. And it means developing a way for each to support and otherwise assist the other with those difficulties.

For most people, taking real initiative in relationships provides a necessary contradiction to early feelings of powerlessness. The pull to set up a socializing-type relationship with a Co-Counselor is a good example of how strong these feelings can be. However much it may feel like a "shortcut" out of your distresses, or a way to avoid difficult issues in a relationship with a non-

counselor, it colludes with feelings of victimization and neediness. The effort to take charge
and set up a situation that works well (with a
non-Co-Counselor) is one of the best contradictions to early abuse.

Any sexual partner will be pleased to have sessions on sex and even to add sessions to sex if it is
done well. Many people are eager to tell about
their early experiences with sex. Sharing life
stories about sex and relationships is a good way
to get a picture of a person's difficulties. It is
important information to use when deciding to
deepen a relationship—do you think you can
handle those particular difficulties? Finding ways
to laugh can be very helpful. If sex is a helpful
contradiction for your non-RC partner, then there
will be opportunities to enhance that contradiction. If sex is difficult, then you can slow down
the action, encourage initiative, and provide
reassurance, good listening, and so on. If at all
workable, each partner should have an
opportunity to set up the situation in a way most
helpful to him or her.

Each relationship is unique, and what will
make each relationship work well is different.
The main ingredient, however, is the ability of at
least one partner (preferably both) to think
freshly about their situation. Following other
models is of limited value. For instance, the question of monogamy must be decided by each

person or couple in the context of their own relationship and the distresses carried by each.

Many people try to base their relationships on how they would like things to be rather than on the actual situation. However, deciding that a situation *should be* workable may be very different than it actually being workable. Whether or not something is ultimately "rational" does not necessarily mean it makes sense in the short run. Any relationship, but especially a sexual relationship, can be viewed as an ongoing "project" which changes over time and which requires thought to keep it moving in a re-emergent direction for all involved.

CHOOSING A PARTNER

Choosing a partner can be an aware process. It need not be left to chance or romantic illusions. People need to face that any real-life mate will have difficulties which will need to be overcome for the relationship to work well. The idea that one should search for a ready-made "perfect" partner needs to be challenged. At some point, a choice needs to be made.

Each person can determine what key features are necessary for an intimate relationship to work well for him or her. Certainly liking a person, having your attention out much of the time you are together, and at least potentially being able to handle the person's difficulties are good places to start. (There will usually be difficulties which feel too tough to handle.)

Some people find themselves under intense family, societal, or peer pressure to "settle down" with a partner. Each person deserves a chance to make this choice for herself. Many people need an opportunity to live on their own and fully "take care of" themselves for a while when they are free to leave their families. Many need a chance to gain experience in relationships with a variety of people. And others may need some time to recover from early hurts so they can take charge of making a relationship work well. It is especially helpful for a person who has just ended a relationship to take some time to clear out related distresses. Otherwise the same difficulties will eventually show up in future relationships.

A preoccupation with intimate relationships can take over many people's lives for a wide variety of reasons. This may be fine for a limited time at the beginning of a new relationship, as partners are getting to know each other up close. However, although regular closeness and affection are important, a special relationship should operate as a support for each person to function increasingly well in a wider and wider sphere. Otherwise, difficulties in taking charge elsewhere will distort and limit what can occur within the relationship, and the relationship will tend to limit each person's life.

ABUSIVE RELATIONSHIPS

Relationships where one person is repeatedly abused, often physically, by the other involve a particular "hooking" of patterns. It becomes obvious from the outside that the abused partner cannot handle the difficulties in the relationship, yet keeps hoping to do so. This must be an exact recording from childhood. Among other things, there is often real caring involved, as well as a need for the physical closeness present in the relationship. Such people can hear the notion of "taking charge of a relationship" as encouragement to stay in a relationship which they cannot handle and which is clearly harmful to them. (This situation is different from simply *feeling* abused.) In such a case, they need assistance to face the situation, end it, and recover from the distresses which make it difficult to have the kind of relationships they want.

AIDS

Being able to think and communicate about at least some aspects of sex has become a life and death issue for many people since the start of the AIDS epidemic. Given the range and depth of distresses in the area of sex, the continuing spread of AIDS through unprotected sexual contact should not be surprising. In addition to information about the disease, people need enough help with their feelings so that they can actually think about their situation and the need for using some dependable protection.

Human beings have a wide variety of ways to be close to each other. Sex is one of those ways, which everyone deserves to enjoy. It is a special way of being close which is also laden with difficulties for just about everyone. Co-Counselors have a unique opportunity to understand the basic operation of distresses in this area and to recover from them. In the process, not only can sex and sexual relationships be a fun and satisfying part of interesting lives, but full functioning can be released in many other areas as well.

Cambridge, Massachusetts, USA

RC Early Sexual Memories Workshop
Notes/Reminders/Helpful Hints
for Support Group Leaders
(and all other counselors)

Here are some specific counseling suggestions and information on leading groups, which Early Sexual Memory Workshop support group leaders and other counselors have found useful. Leaders of Early Sexual Memory support groups outside of workshops and other counselors can adapt the information on groups to their own situations.

1. **I HAVE CONFIDENCE IN YOU.** You know how to counsel people well. Counseling people on their earliest sexual memory is just like counseling people well on anything else. Feel free to use everything you know about how to counsel people (and how to lead groups)—you are not limited to the few ways I will have a chance to demonstrate.

2. I expect you to **keep people discharging the distresses of their earliest memory connected to sex.** They can work on other things at other times, and may need to, but they require your persistence to work on this. While working on the earliest memory, many later memories will come to mind. This is just right. Ask the client to share the later memories (with discharge) and then return

to the earliest one. If the client remembers an earlier memory, switch to working on that one.

3. Clients new to this work usually do well to start by **repeatedly telling the story of the memory.** New details will emerge and bursts of discharge will occur at different points in the re-telling. The counselor needs to actively encourage and provide appropriate contradictions throughout. Soon it becomes more useful to pay attention to one specific aspect of the memory at a time, using all possible counseling tools to assist discharge. However, it is useful for all clients to periodically re-tell the incident in its entirety.

4. Effective counseling in this area will often require **contradicting people's general chronic distress** at the same time you work with them on the content of the memory. (These chronic feelings might be feelings of isolation, that no one cares or is interested, of hating attention, of unimportance, guilt, etc.) Ask your client what life was like for them generally during the time of this incident. Tone of voice, facial expression, and posture of counselors and/or client, as well as what both say, can be good counseling tools here.

5. Pointing people's **attention away from the distress** is usually a key aspect of counseling people well. Finding a positive point of view, using a cheerful tone of voice, reminding clients that the incident has been over for a long time, celebrating their survival, imagining a childhood

or life without those hurts (their own childhood or someone else's), contrasting the present with the past, are some possible approaches. This will become even more important after the first couple of sessions at a workshop. *(Aware listening is often the place to start, especially if discharge is occurring.)*

Clients will usually still need to feel and talk about the incident directly. This will happen spontaneously if you, the counselor, provide an effective contradiction to the distress. When the client talks about the incident, it usually makes sense to listen well, using your own caring as the contradiction at this point.

6. Clients will often remember only small bits of a memory, with the rest being in **occlusion**. They can often discharge well using the piece of information that is available combined with the general feeling of distress they experience when directing their attention to it. The counselor's concern is to assist their client to discharge, not to find out exactly what happened.

However, the counselor will often have to contradict years of denial by everyone in the client's environment by asserting that something very hurtful did actually happen to the client. A pleased announcement that "something happened" (to contradict the variety of possible pressures not to tell) and "it's over now" (to contradict the feeling that the danger is still present) can be useful directions for early work on occlusions.

At some point, the client may also have to make an active decision to remember, to undo the early decision not to remember. It is helpful for the counselor to keep in mind that it was an extremely vulnerable and hurting little one who originally occluded the incident, and that ultimately it is this little one who needs to be reached.

Clients can make up a variety of fantasies to promote discharge, for example, fantasies about small, harmless animals ("One day, a bunny rabbit . . ."); wild stories about sexual abuse which happened to some other child totally unrelated to the client; or what they think may have happened to them. The counselor should assume that each story told about the client himself is true, but that it's also fine that the client change it completely on the next re-telling.

Don't necessarily assume that a particular re-telling which produces copious discharge is what actually happened. Encourage clients to make up new fantasies about what may have happened after discharge has stopped. Eventually, the stories will merge. The essential role of the counselor, however, is to assist clients to face the fact that something very hurtful did actually happen to them, regardless of what it may have been.

7. In the **"role-exchange"** technique, the roles in the original hurt experience are "exchanged"; clients take on the "powerful" role and threaten to abuse their counselors generally and in specifically sexual ways. Counselors can also ask their clients to threaten to abuse them in a way which would leave them feeling the way the client feels about themselves generally or in the area of sex in particular. For example, the counselor might direct, "Threaten to do to me whatever would leave me feeling disliked and unattractive sexually." There is no need for the threatened abuse to have any conscious relationship to the actual abuse which occurred, although the relationship usually becomes apparent before long. This can be another effective way to work on occlusion.

8. Clients can also work on **masturbation fantasies.** This may mean telling the story of the fantasy, thinking about it, telling only parts of it, or saying the word "blank" for each word of the story. The amount of discharge and the ability to stay in contact with the members of the group are good guides to how well it's working. Watch for undischarged shame and humiliation, especially when someone moves too quickly to tell the details of the fantasy. It can be helpful to form special men's and women's groups to discharge sexual fantasies. (Many workshops have optional groups before breakfast.)

9. **The nature of the material people are working on may affect how they relate both to the group and to what they are working on.** They will probably not realize that this is happening. For example, heavy discouragement about ever getting help from you, the group, or the workshop, is likely to be the discouragement about ever getting help which *they experienced during the incident*. Not feeling that they like anyone, wanting to stop, or "needing" to leave, is probably how they felt back then. And any attempt to resist you and your counseling of them is almost always due to the urge (and need) to resist the perpetrator of the early hurt. (Some of these early hurts may still be occluded.) As long as you are clear about what is going on, they can effectively work on how it feels in the present for a while, but it is usually best to relate it to the early memory before too long.

10. **The nature of the material YOU are working on may affect how you relate to the group and how you feel about leading it.** Get someone to listen to you for a few minutes outside of the group and ask yourself how these feelings relate to the feelings from your early memory. (Your group may not be able to stay clear about the actual source of your feelings, so you need to use your judgment about being negative about the group with the group.)

11. A big challenge is to **reserve the bulk of your group time for discharging on the earliest**

memories connected to sex, while taking enough time for other matters that make that work go well—for example, getting to know each other, staying on top of the difficulties at the workshop, and helping people keep their attention out. There is sometimes a pull NOT to get to work, which you will need to contradict (i.e. get people down to work) once people have enough attention to make that work productive.

Suggestions for handling other needs:

•A brief go-around on what's going well at the workshop and any difficulties; if there are difficulties, arrange for the person to get help with the difficulty OUTSIDE OF THE GROUP, whether by you or someone else. Usually, that will be enough. If not, give them a couple of minutes on the "present time" upset, then guide them (gently or otherwise) to work on the early memory—they will usually be related.

•Give everyone a chance to share brief information about themselves and how they may feel different from others in the group. You may want to spread this out over several groups.

•Depending on your particular group, you may need to leave a couple of minutes in between each person's turn for "attention out" activities.

12. **The late afternoon groups are sometimes "harder" than the morning.** (Support groups usually meet two times each day at Early Sexual Memory workshops.) People may be tired, have less energy, less attention, etc. *YOU* may be tired, etc. Try to think about this and set a direction for yourself before the group so you can provide a tone that will contradict any of the other feelings. (A five-minute group cuddle/nap can work well, or sharing about people's lives, singing, etc.)

People may require better, different, and/or more active counseling in the late afternoon groups than in the morning. They have had a session since you saw them last, and a break. If those went well, they may be ready to work on things from a different angle. If those times didn't go well, you may need to provide more of a contradiction to discouragement or other feelings, and pay more attention to their balance of attention.

13. **For some people, long turns work best.** You may want to divide up the group time to make that possible, but make sure everyone gets some kind of a turn at least each day. Sometimes it will make sense to keep a session going longer than planned, with that time being taken off a later turn.

14. **There is at least one other person in your group who we thought could think about the group and you well.** You are encouraged to con-

sult with someone else from your group about counseling people, and to tell that person ahead of time what you need from him or her as your counselor.

15. You should assume **you will do all the counseling** unless **you** think there is a good reason not to (which is fine). You will have a chance to get help with any difficulties as a counselor during the leaders' meetings each day.

16. Get someone else in your group to take leadership for any **work responsibilities** your group may have.

17. **Thank you for taking on this leadership. I depend on you to watch out for the people in your group and to assist them to have a useful workshop.** Get help from someone in their Community or me if you are concerned about anyone.

18. **ENJOY YOURSELVES.** You were chosen because we knew you would do a good job and because we thought the challenge of leading a group would be good for YOU.

—*Joan Karp*